The Book of the Green Man

By the same author:

A Line of Poetry, a Row of Trees (1965)

Sports & Divertissments
(Translations from Erik Satie) 1966

The Book of the Green Man

Then cam four grett wodyn
with four grett clubes all in grene

& with skwybes
borning . . .

by

Ronald
Johnson

New York
W · W · NORTON & COMPANY · INC ·

First Edition

Library of Congress Catalog Card No. 66-18075

Published simultaneously in Canada by
George J. McLeod Limited, Toronto

The *Winter* and *Summer* sections of this poem have appeared in the *Tri-Quarterly Review*, *Spring* appeared in *Poetry* (Chicago), and *Autumn* in *The Lugano Review*.

Printed in the United States of America

2 3 4 5 6 7 8 9 0

For Jonathan & for Dorothy

who made it possible

Contents

The Book of the Green Man

Of the seasons,
seamless, a garland.

Solstice
to equinox—
days,

measured a cock's stride,
come full circle.

The length of
breath,
a sequential foliage

firmly planted in
our veins,
we stand in our rayed form:

blue-eyed,
a chicory,

Sponsa Solis—

& upon the sun appears
a face
also with rays

in descent
through an undulant

blue.

WINTER

. . . Visionary power
Attends the motions of the viewless winds,
Embodied in the mystery of words:
There, darkness makes abode, and all the host
Of shadowy things work endless changes.

William Wordsworth

1

Tchink, Tchink. Tsee!
Then low,
continuous warbles

pure as a Thrush.
A maze
of sound!

The Rothay, deliquescent
somewhere
in these airs

& the sinuous yews.
Tsee!

There is a blinding
darkness, here,

in Grasmere Churchyard

with the movement
of yews, blackbirds & River Rothay
running,

as it has
a hundred years

past Wordsworth's grave-side
—Wordsworth

who could not see
daffodils
only

'huge forms', *Presences* & earth 'working

like a sea'.

It was Dorothy
who lies

at his side,
who brought home

lichen & cushions of
moss,
who saw

these Lakes
in all their weathers—

'dim mirrors',
'bright slate'

—the sheens like herrings
& spear-shaped
streaks

of polished steel.

For William
there was only
one

wind off
the Lakes—

that, that had no
boundary, but entered

'skiey
influences'
into his pores

to animate some inner country
of deep, clear Lakes.

Windermeres
of his mind's eye.

As I sit in this darkness,
the Rothay hissing

like its geese

& the night
forming itself

into shapes of yew

& blackbird songs,

I wish
for this earth, beneath,
to move, to issue some dark, meditated

syllable perhaps—

something more
than this inarticulate

warble
& seething.

But this soil, once
Wordsworth, lies
in silence.

I wish
to make something circular,
seasonal, out

of this 'wheel' of
mountains
—some

flowering thing in its
cycle—an image of our footsteps

planted in homage

over each ridge

& valley.

But having come
to Grasmere,

from where the Lakes radiate
like spokes,

I see only the descent

to this darkness—

the rest
vanishes

—the steaming breath of sheep,

high, upon the fells:

the view
from Great Tongue
to Silver How—

a cone of light, thickening
to greys
down its slopes

—& down
by a ghyll lined with
rowan. Red-berry

—waterfall.
A rising mist to meet us.

Down, to
the quickly darkening
Lake.

The burning blues
of Dove Cottage
garden—

the spectral
October flowers
of night

—hydrangea,
gentian.

This soil, once
Wordsworth . . .

O,
let us give stems to
the flowers!

Substance to this
fog: some

subtle, yet enduring mold,

a snare

for bird-song,

night, & rivers flowing.

Let us catch
the labyrinthine wind,
in words—

syllable, following
on syllable,

somewhere in these airs, these

sinuous yews

—*Gentian, Great Tongue, Westmorland,*
England:

out of this soil, once
Wordsworth . . .

Tsee! Tsee!
Then low,

continuous warbles,
pure,
as a Thrush.

2

I slept
& dreamed
the encircling Mountains

moved toward me in
my sleep.

To the horizon,
the grass
was a deep indigo:

waving & sparkling with hidden
lights.

The edges
of the Mountains moved
slowly,

against the stars,
& there were

sounds as of great doors
opening

as their bases bit

into earth.

I lay
on the sublime motions
of the grasses

& saw stars
descend like snow,

through snow-white brightness

of the skies—

'as if
the Sun shined

for the Snow is reflected
by the Air

just as Fire by Night

is'.

And as the grass grew higher,
I entered into
its Maze—

as of a field of infinite
hoar-frosts melting

& reforming in
shapes

of beasts & curious

vegetation.

I traced

the convolutions of

turf, laid out by men,

& made new windings with the mole

through undisturbed

barrows.

I entered the architecture of

bees—the gold of

their mossed bodies

linked in warmth.

I followed

the patterns of waters

within earth,

& saw the whorls of buried

shells.

I followed the mottled lizard into

scrolls of leaves

& traced the plover to its

nest.

And came, at last, to pastures

where the spiders

had built

on every bush—

that intricate webbing

to which the 'dew

doth perch'.

And on webs, more

tenuous

than these, & of even more

complexity—

the interweavings

of man with earth: warp & woof with

the stuff of Mountains—

I retraced my steps around

the Lakes:

encompassing

Ullswater,

Derwent, Crummock, Buttermere,

Ennerdale, Wastwater,

Conniston, Esthwaite,

Windermere to Elterwater, Rydal, & finally

in a circle back

to Wordsworth & Grasmere.

And this, where I began, was the center
of the Maze:

where the blackbird still sang—its song more
clear

into the night, than any
words—
with the boundless

ambiguity,
ceaseless turnings &

redoubling
& 'motions

of the viewless

winds'.

3

The Oak of the Maze

Lichen.

Lion's shin, oak-limb, tomb:
all acquire
a hundred years'

skin,
a winter's pelt—bones

that 'being
striken one against
another

break out
like fire

& wax greene'.

Mistletoe. Its seeds
ripened
within birds—

out of the quickening gut,
it clings to oak.

An aerial
green,

white-berried.

Ivy. Springs out
of earth,
to cover it

with dark, shining leaves.

It is the mythic coat
of an oak—

made of a shining
& dark-
leaved thunder,

lightnings
& the owls

of its hollows.

There are connections in these

—between an earth, sentient with moles,
& the owl's
radiant eyes—

fine as a web drawn
by spiders,

close as the grain of oak . . .

from earth, to mistletoe, ivy & lichen, to owl's-
wing, to thunder, to lightning, to earth—& back.

There are many ways

to look at an oak, & one, with its
own eyes:

the blunt, burning push
of acorns

in an earth full

of movements, slight rustlings, as a passage of night-birds,

& bones

that ‘being striken one against another

break out like fire

& wax greene’.

SPRING

April 12, 1875

The morning had become grey and overcast, but . . . as we glided up the valley, sweeping round bend after bend we saw new prospects and beauties still unfolding and opening before us, distant azure mountains, green sunny bursts and dark blue wooded hollows of the nearer hills with gentle dips and dimpling swells on the hillsides softly bosoming. Then suddenly came a vivid flash, dazzling with a blaze of diamond sparks thrown off as if by a firework, on the stream suddenly caught and tangled amongst broken rocks, swept roaring in a sheet of white foam through the narrowing channel, or with a stately and gracious bend the river broadened, peaceful and calm, to a majestic reach, long and silver shining, veiled here and there by fringing, overhanging woods and broken by the larch spires dawning a thickening green.

Francis Kilvert

1

Evocations

'Rise, and put on your foliage'.

Come, as the Green Knight to Gawain at the beginning
of the new year—

out of his oaken crevice:
lhude sing cuccu!

Move with a spring & vegetable swiftness,
seed-case & burr & tremulous grasses, a grove—vocal in the wind—

('the rustling of the leaves and
the songs of birds denoting his presence there')

cuckoo!

('at thes day we in ye
sign call them Green Men, covered with green bones')

cuckoo!

('I have listened to the cuckoo in the ivy-tree,
I have listened to the note of the birds

in the crest of the rustling oak,
loud cuckoo')

cuckoo!
cuckoo!

Rise as the sun: antlered—
bearded with greenery—the leaf-vein pulsing

in your throat. Budded all over with small flame, & motley
with birds in your hair & arms. *Rise,*

& put on your foliage!

2

April 8th

We began today
to trace the course
of the Wye

into 'Wild
Wales', Chepstow to Plynlimmon—

limestone bed & cliff—

forest & grassy source.

And as I write this, tonight, at St. Briavels
—a castle squat as a toad, with a moat full of primroses—

I invoke the Wye itself
to cut these pages: its Celtic loops & interlacements,

its continuities that lead the view

onward, & back

to Kilvert—Vaughan.

The echoes of its slow rush ever to be
listened for
in Watershed . . .

Greensward & Sheep . . .

O wind your waters through my song, green Wye.

We first saw the river,
tidal at the Severn, an indefinite
expanse

in morning haze.
Its castle, an extension of the cliff,

an eyrie of
rock, dissolved in the muted,

aerial

greys.

From there up Wyndcliffe, wooded with huge oaks, where the eyes
soar, like birds buoyed up in air:

from the oak-tops—coral & willow with first leaf
& tassle—to clusters of mistletoe

& rookeries, down to gnarled boles slanting against wind
& covered with growths

of ivy, to the carpet of wood-anemone (wood-
anemones, Flowers-Of-The-Wind),

out, over the Wye turning through valleys of
mists, 800 feet below.

Lambs bleating, an 'exaltation'
of larks.

A steady, hushed flow.

Then descended
afoot,

fields bounded with hedge,

each bud & thorn
pendant with
water,

to Tintern—

not one tufted column, no wall
a mass of moving foliage. Only—the Window.

Its seven delicate shafts
the frame for a more ephemeral world
than glass:

the passing clouds,
the passing, voluminous, green clouds—

in hilly

horizon.

Then, leaving the river, over the hill, to St. Briavels.

The wind off
Wyndcliffe

& the spiraling out of sight

of larks in flight.

O wind your waters through these songs, & mine—

river Wye,

green Wye.

3

April 12th

Two days of mossy mists,
soft & clinging. The river, a single grey thread
to be followed through other greys.

Quiet brown blurs
of Hereford cattle, shadowy
swans.

Only the harsh clamor of rooks penetrates.

Though once, a dead sheep floated downstream, every curl,
of its coat, distinct as the bubble

in a house-of-spittle.
Its head like a withered apple.

Today, the Black

Mountains

are a smoke

you could put your hand through

& celandines reflect

the light back like mirrors.

We stopped at Moccas, where Kilvert wrote:

'Those grey
old men of Moccas—

those grey, gnarled, low-browed, knock-kneed,
bowed, bent, huge, strange,
long-armed, deformed, hunch-backed, misshapen oak men—

that stand with both feet in the grave,
yet seeing out,

with such tales to tell,
as when they whisper to each other,
nights,

the silver
birches weep, poplars
& aspens shiver

& long ears of the hares
& rabbits stand

on end'.

And a sparkling snow—from somewhere—through sunshine—

appeared

in clear air.

The Moccas church of
tufa. North Door *carved with a Beast eating*

the Tree of Life, & the South, *with Beast seen devouring a man*

who holds the Tree of Life, the branches of which
form a cross.

And close by, Bredwardine, where Kilvert lies buried.

Where from his grave, 'bright

shootes':

daffodil, primrose, snow-drop, white violet.

4

Emanations

'I am a walking fire, I am all leaves'.

'I find I incorporate gneiss, coal, long-threaded moss,
fruits, grains, esculent roots.
And am stucco'd with quadrupeds & birds all over'.

I find I advance with
sidereal motions
—my eyes containing substance

of the sun,
my ears built of beaks & feathers—

I ascend with saps

& flower in season

& eddy with tides.

With every moon,
I come from the darkness into incandescence.

My tongue assumes the apple's flesh
& my skin, the infinite spheres of the thistle's prickle. And as I
breathe

the wind has its billow—& all the grasses—

in a combing, mazy movement.

5

April 13th

Here, the river swept great
curves
along wide valleys.

We left our footprints

green, behind,
as we followed the straight bright dew-path, meadow banks gleaming.

Clouds moved down the valley—their shadows
a river of huge dapples—their glowing masses opening above
as we came,

a white, enveloping progression.

Mid-day, whole
clouds lowered

& one leaned into wind to walk—
a brisk,
wet fog blowing—

though by evening the sun set westward
in our eyes

among slow cumulus that shafted bands of yellow
light

& remained black spaces
neither earth,
nor air,

suspended in that 'vacant interlunar cave'

where all the stars

revolved, wheeled, glittered.

6

Apparitions

'I thought I saw an angel in an azure robe
coming towards me across the lawn,

but it was only the blue sky through the feathering branches
of the lime'.

7

April 15th, Easter Sunday

We walked in rain
to Llansantffread

—Vaughan buried at St. Bridgit
(the Saint of Light,

born at sunrise on the first day of spring) on
the Usk (as *Vaughan,*

the Swan of). Inside, a font of yellow

sallow,

white iris

& freesia the color of ivory.

' . . . With what floures
And shoots of glory, my Soul breaks'. 'Living bowers'.

Silex Scintillans
these mountains—

the Black & Brecon Beacons

—a deep but dazzling darkness. Beckoning . . .

dissolving,

to white cloud,

& swan, & clod.

Everything,

one river running . . .

8

April 18th

For two days it has rained
& the Wye has been
swollen & brown.

But today it is both clear
& warm, & suddenly, everywhere, all things
are green.

The river, narrowed to a stream,
is a current of long mosses. The trees are fleshed out
with leaf.

There is a constant burbling of curlews.
Crwee, crwee: thick, Welsh consonants, blending with the shallows
of the Wye on rock.

Lambs kick up their heels,
as the bracken unfurls. And as we walk onward, the high, round
hills come with us all the way—

rising into the distance—each one more blue than
the other—out to the long slope
of Plynlimmon. To the sea. *O run slowly, Wye, & evergreen,*

& never end . . .

9

Landscapes & Mandrakes

Then came, like the Celtic Blodeuwedd,

who was made of blossoms of oak

& broom & meadow-sweet,

a green man out of Wales—of more than flowers:
as if all Hafod

rose up again, & came in strides of vistas into England.
And Hafod, that most
sublime of gardens, gone into earth

these hundred years.

And with those lost romantic
promontories, prospects, vapors & auroras,
rolling

& losing themselves in irregularities,
was the half-legendary Wales of Giraldus, where a man could command

the birds to sing: '& immediately the birds,
beating the water with their wings, began to cry aloud

& proclaim him'.

And farther back in time,
the lineaments clearly discerned of
Lothlórien—

of the *mallorn* trees—& shades

of the Blessėd Isles.

And immediately the birds, beating the water with their wings,

began to cry

aloud & proclaim him:

'each grain of

sand, every stone on the land,

each rock & each hill, each fountain & rill,

each herb & each tree, mountain, hill,

earth & sea, cloud,

meteor & star, are men seen

afar'

& near . . .

10

April 19th

Cuckoo . . . cuckoo . . . cuckoo . . .

I had been listening for the first cuckoo, Delius' cuckoo—

but the sound is softer, more penetrant. 'Calling

about the hills', Kilvert says. Yes,

it is that. An echo . . . :

this green source, this welling-forth in ever-widening circles,

this 'spring'.

SUMMER

As the morning advanced the sun became bright and warm, cloudless, calm, serene. About nine an appearance very unusual began to demand our attention—a shower of cobwebs falling from very elevated regions, & continuing, without any interruption, till the close of the day . . .

There is a natural occurrence to be met with upon the highest part of our down in hot summer days, and that is a loud audible humming of bees in the air, though not one insect is to be seen . . .

In a district so diversified as this, so full of hollow vales and hanging woods, it is no wonder that echoes should abound. Many we have discovered that return a tunable ring of bells, or the melody of birds; but we were still at a loss for a polysyllabical, articulate echo, till a young gentleman, who had parted from his company in a summer walk, and was calling after them, stumbled upon a very curious one in a spot where it might least be expected . . .

We procured a cuckoo, and cutting open the breastbone and exposing the intestines to sight, found the crop lying as mentioned above. This stomach was large and round, and stuffed hard, like a pincushion, with food, which upon nice examination, we found to consist of various insects, such as small scarabs, spiders, and dragon-flies; the last of which, as they were just emerging out of the aurelia state, we have seen cuckoos catching on the wing. Among this farrago also were to be seen maggots, and many seeds, which belonged either to gooseberries, currants, cranberries, or some such fruit . . .

All nature is so full, that that district produces the greatest variety which is the most examined . . .

Gilbert White

1

Upon First Opening a Cuckoo

I saw the sweet-briar & bon-fire & strawberry wire now

relaxed into intricate thicket.

It was as if seen in strong sunlight, flat

& tapestried, all edge & definition. Here, an airy bone shaped

like a plowshare, there, vibratory membranes within a space

from which the song must come: a *syrinx* (hollow

pipes of reeds) now silent

in return to the 'Salliter' of earth.

Little more than

a drift of air, brought

into form by plumes.

Mulch to stone.

Yeast of the clouds.

2

What the Earth Told Me

No surface is allowed to be bare,

& nothing to stand still. A man could forever study a pebble

& at last see dilations & expansions of the hills—

to pull the most slender stalk, is to jostle the stars,

& between the bearded grass

& man 'looking in the vegetable glass

of Nature', is a network of roots & suckers

fine as hairs.

I threw a stone upon a pond

& it bounded the surface, its circles interlacing

& radiating out to the most ephemeral edge.

Flint & Mica, Lichened Limestone, Shale & Sarcens, Sandstone, Soil.

I saw the wind moving on a meadow

& the meadows moving under wind—

lifting, settling & accumulating.

Flint & Mica, Lichened Limestone,

Shale & Sarcens, Sandstone, Soil.

3

What the Air Told Me

It is breathed into Orpheus' lyre & as rocks & trees & beasts

is divided there. Its original strain

precedes the sound, by as much as echoes follow after:

the quivering of 'cow-quake', a 'loud audible

humming of bees on the down', stresses within the sustaining earth,

clouds of *fleece* & *mare's tail.*

I saw with single eye, the facet of the fly—

the infinitesimal mechanics & all the metallic sheens

of a blue-bottle. In a land where the sun grows fat on cloud

& *summer hasn't come*

till your foot can cover twenty daisies,

she came to the dark, open beak

& laid a myriad of eggs. And in two day's time the dead

bird's body simulated life: maggots in eye-socket &

under feather, in a subtle movement.

The White & The Glistening.

4

What the Leaf Told Me

Today I saw the word written on the poplar leaves.

It was 'dazzle'. *The dazzle of the poplars.*

As a leaf startles out

from an undifferentiated mass of foliage,

so the word did from a leaf—

A Mirage Of The Delicate Polyglot

inventing itself as cipher. But this, in shifts & gyrations,

grew in brightness, so bright

the massy poplars soon outshone the sun . . .

'My light—my dews—my breezes—my bloom'. Reflections

In A Wren's Eye.

5

De Vegetabilibus

For there are splendors of flowers called DAY'S EYES in every field.

For one cannot walk but to walk upon sun.

For the sun has also a stem, on which it turns.

For the tree forms sun into leaves, & its branches & saps

are solid & liquid states of sun.

For the sun has many seasons, & all of them summer.

For the carrot & bee both bless with sun,

the carrot beneath the earth & the bee with its dusts & honies.

For sun has stippled the pear & polished the apple.

6

De Animalibus

For there are owls in the air & moles in the earth

& THEY ALSO have eyes.

For there are shapes of air which are OWL

& shapes of earth which are MOLE,

& the mole brings air to the earth & the owl, earth into air.

For the turtle's back is another firmament & dappled like the cloud.

For there are birds who nest on the earth

& are feathered in its form.

For the rook & the worm are only one cycle out of many.

For man rejoices with rook & worm

& owl & mole & turtle,

& they are only one cycle out of many.

7

Turner, Constable & Stubbs

To see, Turner had himself lashed to the ship's mast

& Constable sat still in the fields

till something came—a bird—'some living thing appropriate to

the place'. He noted the wind's direction, pile

of clouds, the time of day. Stubbs

fixed an iron bar to the ceiling of his room, with hooks

of various sizes & lengths, in order to suspend the body of a horse.

The horse remained for six or seven weeks

'until no longer endurable'.

The form of muscles, blood vessels & nerves was retained

by tallow injections—Stubbs methodically

cutting to the skeleton, making full length drawings

& studies of the ear & nose.

'He was possessed of great physical

strength, being able,

it is said, to carry a dead horse on his back

to a dissecting room,

at the top of a narrow flight of stairs'.

The work was finished in eighteen months.

8

Natural Productions, Occurrences & Antiquities

'August is by much the most mute month', yet,

the air may be so strongly electric

that bells may ring & sparks be discharged in their clappers:

'put a bird in motion, *et vera incessu patuit* . . . '

To distinguish a bird by its 'air', to 'hear'

the buoyant owls—woodpeckers rising & falling in curves

—the perpendicularity of skylarks . . .

Gilbert White quotes from the Latin: *He preferred*

the sounds of birds to those of men. The music of men left his mind

disturbed by engaging his attention

with its rise & fall, while the warbling

of birds left no such hold

'to tease my imagination & recur irresistibly

at seasons . . . '

All day the cobweb fell silently

in the air, till whole

baskets-full lay round about, & still

more descending.

9

The Leaves of Southwell

Maple & hawthorn & oak. Crow-foot & cinquefoil
(Aubrey's Midsummer Silver?).

Vine & ivy & hops. Rose, bryony (a Mandrake), geranium, mulberry,
wormwood. Fig, bittersweet & blackthorn.

It is an assemblage (a community?) including its dragons with
crisply carved acorns.

Two hounds devour a hare. A bird seizes a grape with its
beak. Both green men & the winged

fruit of maple are in hierarchy of accuracy—the ribbed & the delicate
ascending to the general. But here, a throat

come aleaf, there a branch held aloft.
And a kind of greening speech comes from those mouths

all but winged—each leaf
cleft & articulate. Southwell, of the leaves

of limestone: trefoil, quatrefoil, cinquefoil (as *foil* means
leaf): a 'burnisht corall' & geranium

brain: cranesbill, crow-foot: blackthorn & whitethorn,
quickthorn, Jack-in-the-green:

a man cleft, as Mandrakes, the 'man-shaped
dragon', *Mandragora.*

10

Exhibit from Frederik Ruysch's Anatomical Museum

A skeleton balances an injected spermatic plexus
in one hand & a coil of viscera
in the other. Minatory assortments

of calculi of all sizes
occupy the foreground. In the rear, a
variety of injected vessels, backed by an inflated & injected

tunica vaginalis,
combine to form a grotesque & arboreal
perspective. Another skeleton,

in extremis, is grasping a skeleton
of that emblem of insect mortality, the mayfly, & a third
is performing

a composition 'expressing the sorrows of mankind'
on a violin, symbolized
by bundles of arteries & a fragment

of necrotic femur.
Bones are arranged to represent
a cemetery—wrists are adorned with organic & injected

frills—& human, comparative
& pathological exhibits
are mingled, as the exigencies of space required.

'Unless the Humming of a Gnat is as the Music of the Spheres

& the music of the spheres is as the humming

of a gnat . . . ' A spectre came, *transparent-winged*,

out of the interstices of light,

& shadow went up like smoke & everywhere

the hills were as clouds over valleys of water, rippling

& reverberating.

And before him the sands of the beach swarmed as insects, close-knit

in electrical flight . . .

'For MATTER is the dust of the Earth,

every atom of which is the life.

For the flames of fire may be blown thro musical pipes'.

And everywhere the hills were as clouds over

valleys of water, rippling

& reverberating.

12

What the Light Told Me

It is now a circle, now a spiral or wheel.

It merges with the eye, with a wing or a sickle-shaped horn.

It takes on the form of beasts—a dragon, fish or bird.

As an orb, at summer solstice,
it balances on the altar-stone at Stonehenge—

& as beam, expands, elongates, twists & 'attenuates
itself into leafen gold
as a covering for the quince'.

With arc & parabolic
& serpent-oblique—'musical in ocular
harmony'. Expanding, elongating, twisting
& attenuating.

An encompassing eye.
Within and out, round as a ball—
With hither and thither, as straight as a line.
Slight as a fox-whisker,
spiraled, twined—rayed as chicory-flower.

Within and out, round as a ball—
With hither and thither, as straight as a line.
With lily, germander
And sops-in-wine. With sweet-briar and
Bon-fire and strawberry wire
And columbine.

AUTUMN

Creation sometimes pours into the spiritual eye the radiance of Heaven: the green mountains that glimmer in a summer gloaming from the dusky yet bloomy east; the moon opening her golden eye, or walking in brightness among innumerable islands of light, not only thrill the optic nerve, but shed a mild, a grateful, an unearthly luster into the inmost spirits, and seem the interchanging twilight of that peaceful country, where there is no sorrow and no night.

Samuel Palmer

A chryselephantine sky. The round earth
on flat paper. 'The clouds which drop fatness
upon our fields & pastures'.

Islands—*eye-lands*—& piled mountains
of light. A circumambient voyage into the visible.

I saw that at Shoreham.

I saw hybernacula move
like clouds, & the turtle's eyes red
within.

I saw a badger root among soft
yellow plums of moonlight, & at dawn, a sheep
shake the dews
from its coat, in coronae.

I saw 'vegetable gold'
—the light of suns fold in upon itself,
as leaves
of a cabbage—

I watched the elder grow first
green, then white,
then a lustrous black.

'Thoughts on RISING
MOON with raving-mad splendour
of orange twilight glow on
landscape. I saw that at Shoreham'.

Shoreham—the ripeness
—proliferation. 'Excess more abundantly
excessive'. Its whale-shaped
hills, above the valleys of the hops
& apples. Its shepherds of the many-colored sheep.

I saw ascensions, transformations
& flights 'from a leaf
of kale, across the disc of a planet'.

I saw a world of Leviathan
& the thousand repetitions of spore & insect
intermixed.

Shoreham. Autumnal, mercurial.
A world where the skies
dome above, almost so high as to hold
both rising, meridian & setting suns, with moons large
as barn doors.

A land, perpetually coming
to harvest. The light come out of earth,
a heavy hay—& piled up in stooks
beneath the budding, leafing, flowering chestnut.
I saw that at Shoreham.

I saw all that at Shoreham
& more—the 'cherub-turtles'—the *Shining*

Ones, where they commonly walk . . .

2

Most Rich, Most Glittering, Most Strange

The Beetle, of a coppery green & blue.
Feathers of Peacock & Pheasant.
The live flashing Mackerel,
its thin, transparent colors laid

over silver & gold. Its back, blue
& around its gills, greens which take on
casts of blue. Silvery
belly & eyes a hard, jet black.

The white Owls (inhabiting a shell-room
of a Folly in Wiltshire)
their feathers flecked & barred with
colors of straw & dun. Their

silky eyes blinking in the half-
light of pearled Conch, Cowrie & Coral
spray. The Moth, the Mantis,
Dragon-fly. A Snail's path seen shining

in sunlight. Pope's grotto built
at Twickenham, with its Marble of diverse
colors. And between each course of
Marble, many kinds of Ores, such as Tin

Ore, purpled Copper Ores & Wild Lead
intermixed with large clumps of
Cornish Diamonds. Rich,
White Spars interlaced with Cockle

& Spars shot with prisms of
different degrees of waters. Fossils
interspersed with Grains of Mundic:
some yellow, some purple & some deep blue

inclining to black. Crystal from
Germany, Gold from Peru, Silvers from
Spain & Mexico. Gold Clift
from Gloucestershire, Egyptian Pebbles.

Petrified Wood & Moss. Blood-
stones, clumps of Amethyst, 'Isicles'.
Curious stones from everywhere & several
Humming-birds, with nests.

Those opalescent clouds in the form
of scales of fish: striped, undulating,
cirrus-like—with spectral 'eyes'
of a bright, metallic lustre.

Fog-bow & Moon-bow. Haloes observed
around the sun, with Mock Suns, upon days
of peculiar, milky light. Green
'Rays', or Flames, seen to

shoot up, high, above the setting sun.
Multiple Crescents of the moon.
Mirage & iridescence of oil-spots & suns
'Drawing Water'. Moonglade,

Touch-wood. That luminescence,
phosphorescence, fluorescence, to be seen
in plant, animal & stone. Rabbits'
eyes, Will-o'-the-Wisp,

the shimmering hand dipped in warm
waters. The ancient trees
whose every leaf is a streak of
pale flame, the glow of whose roots can

be traced upon earth. The legend
of electrical hail-stones, 'Hercynian'
birds like plumed lamps
lighting the forests at night

& the vine said to entangle cattle's
hooves & horns in networks
of fiery tendril. All things 'most rich,
most glittering, most strange'.

3

Of Certaine White Nights Wherein the Darkes Doe Seem to Gette Up & Walk & How Wee Saw Divers Wonders in Bothe Earth & Element.

As we descended to this valley,
where Samuel Palmer had used to walk—bareheaded
under the moon—
the passing clouds above
'did marvellously supple the ground'.

And there were seen many blackbirds to settle
as shapes of water on the land.

Out of the warm hills at our backs
a nebulous lightning
pulsed & flickered, a false
Aurora Borealis, enfolding us as we came.

Wee had observed
these glows to collect as solid
as stones, at the sides of our eies—

& the hollows,
each, to appear to rise out
of its owne darkeness.

We also came upon one tree,
out of those that abound here, whose leaves
seemed brought into curious relief
by the twilight being reflected upon one
side, & a waxing moon,
on the other—

it is thus our nights, everywhere,

continued
but dusks of daies.

William Stukeley made his own Stonehenge, a Druid Temple 'formed out of an old ortchard'. 'Tis thus', he writes—'there is a circle of tall filberd trees in the nature of a hedg, which is 70 foot diameter & round it a walk 15 foot broad, circular

too, so that the whole is 100 foot diameter. The walk from one high point slopes each way, gradually, till you come to the lowest point opposite, & there is the entrance to a temple, to which the walk may be esteemed as porticoe. When one enters

into this innermost circle or temple, one sees, in the center, an antient appletree oregrown with sacred mistletoe. Round it is another concentric circle of a 50 foot diameter made all of pyramidal greens, at an equal interval, that appear as verdant

when fruit trees have dropt their leaves. The pyramidals are in imitation of Stonehenge's inner circles. The whole of this is included within a square wall on every side, except the grand avenue to the porticoe, which is an appletree avenue. The

angles are filled in fruit trees, plumbs, pears, & walnuts, & such are likewise interspersed in the filberd hedg & borders, with some sort of irregularity to prevent any stiffness in its appearance & make it look more easy & natural. At that point,

where is an entrance from the porticoe to
the temple, is a tumulus, but I must take
it for a cairn, or celtic barrow. I have
sketched you out the whole thing as it is
formed. These are some of the amusements
of country folk, insted of conversation'.

Alexander Pope: 'I have sometimes had the idea of planting
an old gothic cathedral. Good

large poplars with their white
stems (cleared of their boughs
to a proper height) w'ld serve
well for columns, & might form

the aisles or the peristiliums
by their different distances &

heights. These w'ld look very
well near, & a dome rising all
in a proper tuft in the middle
w'ld look well at a distance'.
This is the man whose parodies

of topiary were inimitable, who deplored the
fantastical & wished for 'unadorned
Nature'. But the 'Gothick' was in fashion & has
since been destroyed as
the formal topiary before it—to serpen-
tinize brooks, to make vistas.

Now, the obelisks are toppled,
labyrinth & maze are uprooted to pasture
& ivies hide the Folly.
The giantesque animals, lop-sided arches & cones
& pyramids, have been allowed, now,
to grow into ghosts of shapes they once had.

'A laurestine bear in blossom, with a juniper hunter in berries. A pair of giants, stunted. A lavender pig with sage growing in his belly. The Tower of Babel. St. George in box, his arm

scarce long enough, but able to stick the dragon by next April—the dragon, also of box, with ground-ivy tail. A pair of maiden-heads in fir, in great forwardness. A quickset hog, shot up

to a porcupine, by its being forgot a week in rainy weather. Noah's ark in holly, Adam & Eve in yew—the serpent flourishing. Edward the Black Prince in cypress, an old maid in wormwood'.

5

The Balancings Of The Clouds—their breeze
& darknesses. Wheaten emanations
of earth. A man come piping
over the hills—an interpenetration of
moth-wing & seed-case & burr, of tremulous grasses
& ripening apples.

I saw that at Shoreham.

In the 'yellow spot' of clear vision,
the apples grew & reddened—
the trunk of their tree come suddenly out
of a slope, as Arcimboldo's lemons from a throat.

'Unless the eye
contained the substance of the sun . . . '

Unless the ears are shaped
of song, our nose is of air, our skin, of the thistle,

& our tongue, of apples & water:

'The Apple-Tree, the Singing & the Gold . . . '

It is here
was Hesperides, *Paradisi in Sole*
Paradisus Terrestris.

I held a yellow twilight in my head.
I saw the glow of its after-
image, green & blue, circle the globes of apple.
I walked upon the clods
of cumulus, & saw a 'glory' moving always before me
on the grass. And melody came, in openings

of the air. All
eyes. In Shoreham's Albion. A *Paradys*

Erthely.

6

At 5° altitude of the sun, on a clear

day, the horizon has become warm
yellow, a faintly yellow horizontal stripe

becomes visible below the sun,
& concentrically above is a luminous
white arc. The eastern counter-twilight

is a transition of orange,
yellow, green & blue. At altitude
0°, in the west, the horizontal stripe
becomes white-yellow, yellow

& green. The arching, white transparency
is encircled by brown tones.
In the east, the shadow of earth rises.
It is bluish-grey, shifting to
purple. Above, the counter-twilight

becomes more vivid, & higher still
there is a bright reflection of the light
in the west—a widespread
illumination. At −1° the color
from the earth upwards is brown-orange
fading to gold. The eastern shadow

rises higher & is darker.
The counter-twilight develops a
border of colors shading from violet to
crimson, orange, yellow, green
& blue. And above that—brightness.
At −3° the colors in the east are

at their most vivid & in the west, a rose-
red spot appears above the
white arc. It grows larger & more
diffuse, the color of salmon.
At $-5°$ this has changed to a radiant

purple. Trunks of trees & soil
take on its warm tint & the east becomes
an after-glow of dull reds.
This purple light fades, apparently

mingling with the horizontal striping,
& the boundary of earth-shadow
disappears in the east. Landscape

illumination fails so rapidly it becomes
difficult to see. Imperceptibly

all colors vanish & there is darkness.

THE WHITE CLOUD. There is a sound of thunder
from the sea, over the slate-blue
Kentish hills. Overhead, the blue sky

intensifies its blue & the wheat radiates yellow.
Upper slopes of the cloud-bank
reflect the rays of sun. It is a massive
ridge, its underside a misty black
reaching to the horizon.

A dull booming rolls in from
the south, as if through
solid sunlight.
A warm haze settles over the wheat.

The air is sibilant with
insect wings. In the distance,
several reapers bend
to scythe grain

& all is quickened
with hidden electricity.

The field, with its broken fence,
slopes down to where a thatched barn is half
hidden among beeches.

This is a plain structure, shaped like
a hill. Its roof sags, encrusted
with that emerald-green moss, *Tortula ruralis:*
smooth, rounded clumps—
now, in the dryness of harvest,

partly shrunken, & of a yellow-stained
olive. Three large rooks move slowly above the ripe
stalks unperturbed
by the reapers. A white owl
leaves the barn—whiter still against the dark
valley.

The beeches tremble imperceptibly.
An old, gnarled oak, blasted in the past by
lightning, turns yellow.

The reapers working
against the low rumble
at their backs.
The white cloud still, haze
suspended,

dust from stubble
hanging in the heavy
air, & far
behind the barn a brook
audible.

The dry wheat,
straw warm to the
touch, earth
hot beneath the
foot.

Insect wings. Light feet of squirrels
in the beeches. Rustling of dry leaves on the oak.
Waters. The sunlight in rippling spots as it
plays on the ground. Hues of the swaying wheat
from palest yellows to ruddy gold.
Sheen on the blackbirds. Undertone of thunder.

Dry scrape of grasshoppers. Quick
patter of squirrels. Wind in the oak leaf
& water on stone. A maze of sun dappled over earth.
The straw whispering as it is scythed.
Wings of blackbirds glistening as they settle.
The thunder barely to be heard.

At our backs, surrounding the picture,
is the whole world.

Sun caps the tops of clouds
with silver. Bells in the churches
begin to ring from distant hills.
The moon, rising over a hill, casts long shadows
from a clump
of horse-chestnuts.

A YELLOW MOON, A YELLOW MOON, A YELLOW MOON.
Scents of newly-cut wheat
billow on the night air. An owl
calls—echoes & reverberates around us.
Dimness & brillance meet.
Large stars.

I walked up to the CLOUD,

'a country
where there is no
night'

but of moons
& with heads of fish

in the furrow,

& on each
ear, beneath a husk
of twilight

were as many suns as
kernels,

& fields were far

as the eye
could reach.

Then dipping their silver oars,

the eyes
shed characters of fire
in the grain,

its sheaves as if mackerel
shone on the waves

of air.

I walked up to the CLOUD

& the white light
opened
like flowers—

dog violet,
& asphodel, celandine,

red clover.

I walked up to the CLOUD

& peal after peal
rang out of earth.

First, stones
underfoot
in a sound like muffled

sheep-bells.
Then the roots of the trees

clanged:
rooks, rooks, blackbirds. Cuckoos awoke
in the tubers

—earth-worm & mole & turtle—

all danced to the thunder,
the peal & thunder.

A bellow & clamor
came out
of the hills:

in diapason—a dissonance
& musical order.

ROOKS, ROOKS, BLACK-
BIRDS, CUCKOOS.

EARTH-WORM & MOLE
& TURTLE.

NOTES

Thoreau writes in his Diary for March 16th, 1851: "When I looked into Purchas's Pilgrims, it affected me like looking into an impassable swamp, ten feet deep with sphagnum, where the monarchs of the forest, covered with mosses and stretched along the ground, were making haste to become peat. Those old books suggested a certain fertility, an Ohio soil, as if they were making a humus for new literatures to spring in. I heard the bellowing of bullfrogs and the hum of mosquitoes reverberating through the thick embossed covers when I had closed the book. Decayed literature makes the richest of all soils."

Notes are an encumbrance to poetry, usually, but at the same time I lust after books with a certain 'Ohio soil', a rich silt of bibliography, books which lead to other books. Thus I would hope that these notes will not burden the poetry, but indicate where I, too, have heard the bullfrogs and out of what earths I have tried to cultivate new growth.

Epigraph: Lewis Spence, in *The Minor Traditions of British Mythology*, quotes from Machyn's *Diary* (commenting on a procession at a Lord Mayor's Day, London, Oct. 29th, 1553): "Then cam four grett wodyn [wild men] with grett clubes all in grene, and with skwybes [squibs] borning . . . with gret berds and ryd here and four targets a-pon their bake."

Page 11, line 16: *Sponsa Solis,* a common Latin name for chicory in the fifteenth century.

Page 13, epigraph: William Wordsworth, *The Prelude.*

Page 15, line 25: *The Prelude,* also: ". . . In my thoughts/There was a darkness, call it solitude/Or blank desertion, no familiar shapes/Of hourly objects, images of trees;/Of sea or sky, no colours of green field;/But huge and mighty Forms." Also: "The earth . . . work like a sea."

Page 16, lines 11–16: Dorothy Wordsworth, *Journals.*

Page 16, lines 24–25: William Wordsworth quotes this in *A Guide Through the District of the Lakes . . .*

Page 17, line 24: Wordsworth uses the image of a wheel to describe the mountains of the Lake District in his *Guide.*

Page 22, lines 5–10: Friedrich Martens, *An Account of Several Late Voyages and Discoveries.*

Page 23, lines 20–21: The dew "doth pearche unto the grasse" . . . Richard Surflet, *Maison Rustique, or The Countrie Farme.*

Page 26, lines 7–12: Lyly, *Euphues.* "The bones of the Lyon, which lying still and moved begin to rot, but being striken one against another break out like fire, and wax greene."

Pages 26–27: The Ivy-Thunder-Oak complex is described in Alexander Porteous' *Forest Folklore, Mythology, and Romance.*

Page 29, epigraph: Francis Kilvert, *Diaries.*

Page 31, line 1: Robert Herrick, *Corinna's going a-Maying.*

Page 31, lines 8–9: Alexander Porteous, *Forest Folklore . . .*

Page 31, lines 11–12: Harlein MSS 5900.

Page 31, lines 14–17: Kenneth Jackson quotes this poem in the Welsh section of *Studies in Early Celtic Nature Poetry.*

Page 32, lines 4–5: Taliesin, *Destiny of the Britons:* "Their Lord they shall praise,/Their language they shall keep,/Their land they shall lose/Except Wild Wales."

Page 34: We have forgotten, now, the original inspiration of Tintern Abbey. For a description of its appearance in the eighteenth century one should read Thomas Whately, *Observations on Modern Gardening.*

Page 35, lines 19–20 and Page 36, lines 1–14: Francis Kilvert, *Diaries.*

Page 37, lines 1–2: Henry Vaughan, *The Retreat.*

Page 38, line 1: Edith Sitwell, *The Song of the Cold.*

Page 38, lines 2–4: Walt Whitman, *Song of Myself.*

Page 40, line 1: An interesting example of the power of memory (as well as prose) to improve on poetry is Thomas Gray's recollection of Milton's lines from *Samson Agonistes:* "The Sun to me is dark/And silent as the Moon,/When she deserts the night/Hid in her vacant interlunar cave." Gray wrote in his *Journal* while he was visiting the Lakes: "Wished for the Moon, but she was *dark to me & silent, hid in her vacant interlunar cave.*"

Page 41, lines 1–4: Francis Kilvert, *Diaries.*

Page 42, lines 11–12: Henry Vaughan, *The Morning-watch.*

Page 42, line 12: Vaughan again, from *The Timber.*

Page 45, lines 5–13: Hafod, now completely destroyed, can be read about at its height in George Cumberland's *From an Attempt to Describe Hafod,* and is also the subject of Elisabeth Inglis-Jones' recent book, *Peacocks in Paradise.*

Page 45, lines 15–17: Giraldus Cambrensis, *Itinerary Through Wales.*

Page 45, lines 20–21: No work on England and mythology is complete, I reckon, without some mention of J. R. R. Tolkien's *Book of the Rings,* the most magical imaginative work of the twentieth century.

Page 46, lines 5–11: This is a reconstruction of Blake's poem *To Thomas Butts.*

Pages 49–50, epigraphs: Gilbert White, *The Natural History of Selborne.*

Page 51, line 8: Jakob Boehme, *The Signature of All Things:* "View this world diligently and consider what manner of sprouts, and branches grow out of the *Salitter* of the earth, from trees, plants, herbs, roots, flowers, oil, wine, corn, and whatever else there is that thy heart can find out; all is a type of the heavenly pomp."

Page 51, lines 9–11: John Ruskin, *Athena in the Earth.*

Page 52, lines 6–7: William Blake, *Milton.*

Page 53, lines 10–11: A folk saying.

Page 54, lines 1–2: Francis Kilvert, *Diaries.*

Page 54, line 10: This is quoted from Constable in *John Constable's Clouds* by Kurt Badt (tr. Stanley Godman).

Page 57, lines 3–4: W. P. Frith in *Further Reminiscences* quotes Constable as saying "I always sit till I see some living thing; because if such appears, it is sure to be appropriate to the place."

Page 57, lines 9 and 14–18: *George Stubbs, 1724–1800, Catalogue of an Exhibition, Walker Art Gallery, Liverpool, 1951.*

Page 58, lines 1, 4, and 8–14: Gilbert White, *The Natural History of Selborne.*

Page 59: Southwell Minster is described in Nicholas Pevsner's *The Leaves of Southwell.* The information about plants in this section comes from Geoffrey Grigson's *An Englishman's Flora* (though one should read *all* of Grigson; his books are seminal and essential).

Page 60: This description of Frederik Ruysch's Anatomical Museum comes from Ruthven Todd's *Tracks in the Snow.*

Page 61, title and lines 1–2: Henry David Thoreau, *Journals.*

Page 61, lines 9–11: Christopher Smart, *Jubilate Agno.*

Page 62, lines 6–8: James Hervey, *Meditations and Contemplations.*

Page 62, lines 10–11: Smart again—*Jubilate Agno.*

Page 62, lines 14–15 and 18–23: This is an anonymous song culled from Edith Sitwell's *Book of Flowers.*

Page 63, epigraph: Samuel Palmer, letter to John Linnell, from *Life and Letters of Samuel Palmer*, by A. H. Palmer.

Page 65, lines 2–3: Isaac Barrow, *Sermons on the Creed.*

Page 65, line 14: "The wall-flowers . . . rise in vegetable gold"—John Langhorne, *The Fables of Flora.*

Page 65, lines 21–24: Samuel Palmer, a letter quoted in A. H. Palmer's *Life and Letters . . .*

Page 66, lines 2–3: Also a letter quoted from above.

Page 66, lines 7–8: A. H. Palmer, himself, from the *Life and Letters . . .*

Page 66, line 23: Christopher Smart, *Hymns.*

Page 66, lines 23–24: "For in this land the Shining Ones commonly Walked"—John Bunyon, *The Pilgrim's Progress.*

Page 67, title: I remember this being quoted from Gustave Moreau in *Time* Magazine, but have been unable to trace the quotation.

Page 67, lines 9–10: I must thank Miss Barbara Jones for taking me to this grottoesque folly. It is also fully described in her book *Follies & Grottoes.*

Page 67, lines 17–28 and page 68, lines 1–8: This description of Pope's grotto is arranged, as his apparently was, in a style which could only be termed Formal Willy-Nilly, and comes from Pope's gardener, J. Serle—*A Plan of Mr. Pope's Garden.*

Page 68, lines 9–20: These optical phenomena are explained fully in M. Minnaert's *Light and Color in the Open Air*, a book more useful for poets than painters these days.

Page 68, lines 26–29: These trees grow in George Macdonald's *Phantastes.*

Page 68, lines 30–32: Pliny—"In the Hercynian forests of Germany we have heard there are strange birds whose feathers shine like fire in the night."

Page 69, lines 1–3: *Hutchinson's Popular Botany*, by A. E. Knight and Edward Step, has a section devoted to phosphorescence and luminescence in plants. Among other things they mention "Cipo, a South American Vine, said to be so highly luminous, that, when injured, it seems to bleed streams of living fire. Large animals have been noticed standing among its crushed and broken tendrils, dripping with the gleaming fluid, and surrounded by a seeming network of fire."

Page 70: Title: In a letter to John Linnell quoted by A. H. Palmer in *Life and Letters . . .* Samuel Palmer, in speaking of "the *Night of Michelangelo,*" writes "If the *Night* could get up and walk . . . "

Page 70, line 5: Samuel Purchas, *Purchas his Pilgrimage:* "These waters doe marvellously supple the ground . . . "

Page 70, lines 18–23: "So we went through the aspens at the base of the Cliffs, their round leaves reflecting the lingering twilight on the one side, the waxing moonlight on the other." Thoreau, *Journals.*

Page 72 through page 73, lines 1–6: William Stukeley's description of his Stonehenge "Ortchard" comes from a letter written by him to Samuel Gale quoted in *Family Memoirs of the Rev. William Stukeley.*

Page 73, lines 7–20: *Anecdotes,* by the Rev. Joseph Spence.

Page 74, lines 1–15 and page 50: Alexander Pope, *Guardian, No. 173, 1713.*

Page 75, lines 12–13: "Unless the eye contained the substance of the sun how could we ever look on the light?" Goethe, *Zahme Xenien.*

Page 75, line 17: Euripides, *Hippolytus* (tr. Gilbert Murray).

Page 75, lines 19–20: This is the punning title of a book by Thomas Parkinson (Park-in-sun).

Page 75, lines 2–3: Chaucer, *The Romaunt of the Rose.*

Page 77 through page 78, line 15: This is adapted from M. Minnaert's *Light and Color in the Open Air.*

Page 78, line 16: *The White Cloud* is the title of a picture by Samuel Palmer—its capitalization is an imitation of the way he wrote titles to paintings in his letters.

Page 79, line 8: Geoffrey Grigson's *An English Farmhouse and its Neighborhood* describes these bright clumps of moss that Palmer painted so exquisitely.

Page 80, lines 28–30: see epigraph to the *Autumn* section.

"The Green Man" of the title is not a poetic metaphor, merely, but is still to be seen in England. It is not uncommon for pubs or inns to be called by his name, a hold-over from times when he was a current legend and was deeply associated with Robin Hood, and the Green Knight in *Gawain and the Green Knight.* But he is most often to be found, today, as a face with sad, heavy-lidded eyes occupying the corbel of an arch in churches. There, he has branches growing out either side of the mouth, or is bearded in leaves with more foliage springing from the forehead, or is garlanded.

As King of the May, or Jack-in-the-Green, he has a persistent history that can be traced back to May Day celebrations throughout Northern and Central Europe. Geoffrey Grigson writes that traditionally "on May Day in the village plays and ceremonies he was sacrificed dying for all the death of the plants in winter." In former times he was also marched in the London Lord Mayor's Day Parade enclosed in a wooden framework on which leaves were clustered and from which came explosions of fireworks. Chimney sweeps paraded beneath the same pyramidal frameworks on May Day until the nineteenth century. One imagines them coming like small boxwood topiary, crackling and sparkling through the streets.

Lewis Spence adds a less typical, later variant: "I have seen him at South Queensferry, on the southern shores of the Firth of Forth, where he is known as the 'Burry Man', a boy on whose clothes large numbers of burrs or seed-cases have been so closely sewn that he presents the appearance of a moving mass of vegetation."

He is also seen, of course, in the guise of Arcimboldo's "portraits" of the seasons or as the fanciful Seventeenth Century Gardener pictured in herbals and gardening books in a finery of flowers and of vegetables. Or, the reverse side of a coin, as the Mandrake—a plant forming itself in the shape of man. The hand that seems to sprout leaves at its wrist and is used in this book is a pseudo-mandrake—actually a radish. Its nineteenth century engraver, copying a seventeenth century painting of this miraculous radish, was, perhaps, both over-credulous and over-exuberant. Not only are there illusionistic finger joints, but a thumb-nail as well. *The World Of Wonders, No. 3,* also mentions "another radish, exactly resembling a human hand, in the possession of Mr. Bisset, secretary to the museum at Birmingham, in 1802. He declared in his letter that the fingers were quite perfect, and that a large sum had been offered for it and refused."